Teach Me
SPORTS
S O C C E R

BY BARRY DREAYER

D0559058

GPG

General Publishing Group, Inc.
Los Angeles

Publisher: W. Quay Hays
Editor: Barry Dreayer
Managing Editor: Colby Allerton
Cover Design: Kurt Wahlner
Production Manager: Nadeen Torio
Copy Editor: Charles Neighbors

Special thanks to the following individuals for their assis-
tance with this Soccer Edition: Vicki Blumenfeld, Yaro
Dachniwsky, Jacob Daniel, Roger Gardocki, Dan Herbst, Paul
Joffe, Frank Lango, Charlie Morgan, Kassandra Smolias,
Graham Tutt and Oded Zyssman.

All views and opinions expressed herein are solely those of
the author.

The *Teach Me Sports*™ series is published by General Publishing
Group, Inc., 3100 Airport Avenue, Santa Monica, CA 90405
310-915-9000.

Library Catalog Number 94-075776
ISBN 1-881649-36-9

10 9 8 7 6 5 4 3 2 1

Printed in the USA

INTRODUCTION

Though not as visible in the U.S. as many other professional sports, soccer is the most popular spectator
sport in the world. It is also played by more kids in
this country than any of the other major athletics.
American interest in soccer has been intensified
recently by such major international showcases as the
1994 World Cup (with the final rounds played in
selected U.S. cities) and the 1996 Olympics in Atlanta.

Soccer fans in other countries are known for being
among the most passionate supporters of any sport.
Many will travel very long distances to attend games,
and violent altercations have been common between
legions of opposing fans.

Most readers probably already know that soccer
involves players trying to kick the ball into the opponent's goal. Requiring very little equipment, soccer is
also a game of constant motion that requires players
with great stamina, skill and intelligence. This book
examines the rules, strategies and excitement of soccer.

So, come on and join the fun by learning the game!

Teach Me SPORTS
JOIN THE FUN BY LEARNING THE GAME

THE SOCCER EDITION

THE ORIGIN OF SOCCER

Ball-kicking games have been around for thousands of years. Ancient barbarians in England used the skulls of dethroned Roman conquerors for games of kick-around. Drawings and stories indicate that some sort of ball-kicking games were also a part of early Greek, Chinese, Japanese, Italian and Mexican cultures.

Modern soccer can be attributed to the British. In the 1100s, a ball-kicking game with up to 500 people on each side was played. Frequently, the goals were lines drawn at each end of the village. Monarchs outlawed the game in the 1300s because of its extreme violence, and participants were threatened with imprisonment.

It wasn't until the 1800s that some semblance of order took place. English prep schools enhanced the game's popularity and laid down some rules. To prevent chaos, the most important rule was to limit the size of each team. In 1823, William Webb Ellis (an impatient student at Rugby School) created a controversy by picking up the ball and running with it. Those who favored allowing players to use their hands eventually devised the game that is now called *rugby*.

Others preferred the "hands-less" game which we know today as soccer. Originally, it was called *association football*, then shortened to *assoc*. English schoolboys, for fun, used to add the suffix "er" to the end of most words, so "assocer," or *soccer* was born. Now, in most countries except the United States, the game is referred to as *football*.

In 1904, soccer became so widespread across the world that FIFA (Fédération Internationale de Football Associations) was formed with headquarters in Switzerland. Its purpose was to standardize the rules of soccer. Today, it is still the governing body of soccer and coordinates both the Olympic and World Cup competitions.

The *Teach Me Sports Soccer* edition concentrates on the international rules (*laws* is the formal term) as adopted by FIFA. Some youth (under 16 years old), veteran (over 35) and women's leagues are allowed to modify:

- the size of the field.
- the size, weight and material of the ball.
- the width of the goal posts and height of the crossbar.
- the regulation time of the game.
- substitution rules.

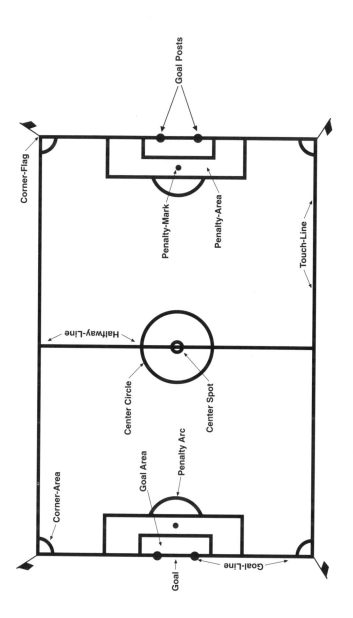

BASIC RULES AND OBJECTIVES

Each team is allowed 11 players on the field at the same time.

- The team that has possession of the ball is the OFFENSE and is the ATTACKING TEAM.

- The team without possession of the ball is the DEFENSE and is the DEFENDING TEAM.

The team that scores the most goals during the regulation time of the game is the winner. If no goals are scored, or if each team scores an equal number of goals, the game is declared a tie or DRAW.

- A GOAL is scored when the entire ball passes over the GOAL-LINE between the GOAL POSTS and underneath the CROSSBAR, provided the ball has not been thrown by or last hit by the hand or arm of a player on offense.

- The regulation time for a soccer game is 90 minutes, divided into two 45-minute periods.

  - Because the scoreboard clock is never stopped during the game, time can be extended in either period if there have been delays.

    1. The delays include time that is spent treating injured players, substituting players and other events that take up time.

    2. When play continues longer than 45 minutes in a half, the teams are playing in ADDED TIME or INJURY TIME.

  - The scoreboard clock stops with 2 minutes left, but play continues for the next 2 minutes plus any added time.

  - HALF-TIME is an intermission that takes place between the 2 periods.

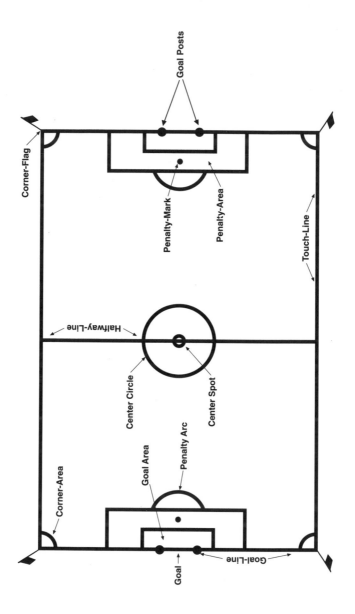

Goal Posts

Corner-Flag

Penalty-Mark

Penalty-Area

Touch-Line

Halfway-Line

Center Circle

Center Spot

Penalty Arc

Goal Area

Corner-Area

Goal-Line

Goal

12

In some tournament games, a DRAW is not acceptable because a single winner (who then advances to the next round or, if it is the final round, is the champion) must be determined. Extra time periods and sometimes a number of penalty-kicks are used to decide the ultimate winner of the game. (See World Cup Championship section.)

Before the start of the game, a COIN TOSS takes place.

- The team that wins the toss has the first option of choosing whether:
  - To KICK OFF (which means to start the game by kicking the ball from the center spot to another teammate into the opposing team's half of the field), or
  - To pick which one of the two goal-lines it will defend.
- The team that did not kick off at the beginning of the game kicks off at the start of the second half.
- The teams switch sides and defend the opposite goal-lines in the second half.

After a goal is scored, the team which gave up the goal kicks off to resume play.

A team is allowed to make only 2 substitutions during a game.

- There are 16 eligible players on each team in a game—11 starting players and 5 extra players of whom 2 may be used as substitutes.
- Once a player is replaced by a substitute, he may no longer play in the game.
- If both substitutions have already been made, and a player becomes injured and cannot continue, the team must play with one less player.

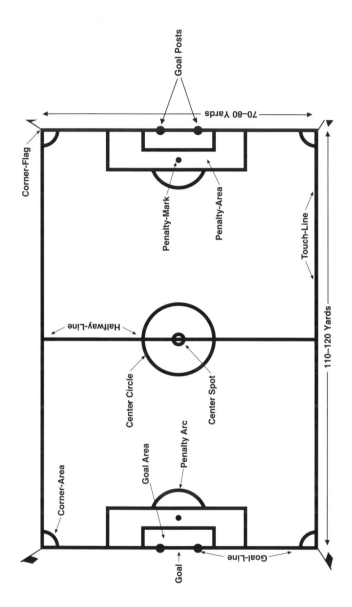

Goal Posts

70–80 Yards

Corner-Flag

Penalty-Mark

Penalty-Area

Touch-Line

110–120 Yards

Halfway-Line

Center Circle

Center Spot

Corner-Area

Goal Area

Penalty Arc

Goal

Goal-Line

14

FIELD OF PLAY

The playing field for international play is rectangular and has the following variable dimensions:

- The length must be between 110 and 120 yards.
- The width must be between 70 and 80 yards.

On each end of the field is the GOAL-LINE, and on each side of the field is the TOUCH-LINE. The lines themselves are considered to be within the field of play ("in-bounds").

GOAL POSTS are centered on each goal-line, 8 yards apart.

- The goal posts are connected by a horizontal crossbar at a height of 8 feet.
- Attached to the goal posts, crossbar and the ground behind each goal-line is a net to "catch" the ball when a goal is scored. The net plays no other significant role in the game.

A rectangular area in front of and including part of the goal-line is called the PENALTY-AREA.

- This area is 44 yards wide and 18 yards deep.
- Each team's GOALKEEPER is permitted to use his hands or arms in handling the ball inside his penalty-area. No other player is allowed to use his hands or arms inside any portion of the playing field.
- The penalty-area defines the section of the field where a major foul committed by the defensive team results in a PENALTY-KICK (discussed in detail in the Terms and Definitions section). The penalty-area includes a mark, 12 yards from the middle of the goal, where the ball is placed for a penalty-kick.

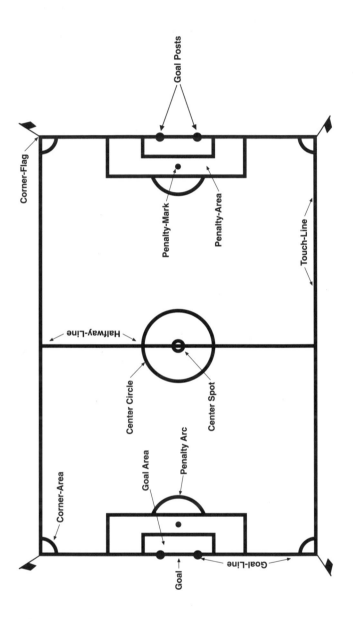

Goal Posts

Corner-Flag

Penalty-Mark

Penalty-Area

Touch-Line

Halfway-Line

Center Circle

Center Spot

Corner-Area

Goal Area

Penalty Arc

Goal

Goal-Line

Within the penalty-area is a smaller rectangular box called the GOAL-AREA.

- The goal-area is 20 yards wide and 6 yards deep.
- One side of the goal-area includes part of the goal-line.
- This area designates where the ball may be placed for a GOAL-KICK (discussed in the Terms and Definitions section). The ball may be kicked from anywhere within the goal-area.

At each corner of the field, a quarter circle is drawn in the field of play, indicating where the ball should be placed for a CORNER-KICK (also discussed in detail later).

A flag is at each corner of the field where the goal-line and touch-line meet. The flags assist in determining if a ball going outside the playing field crosses over the goal-line or the touch-line.

The field is divided in half by the HALFWAY-LINE (parallel to the goal-lines).

- The half of the field that includes the goal-line that a team is defending is referred to as that team's half of the field.
- At the center of the line is a spot where the ball is placed for the kick-off.
- Each team must be on its own side of the halfway-line during a kick-off.
- In the middle of the field is a circle, called the CENTER CIRCLE, which has a 10-yard radius. The defenders must stand outside the center circle on their half of the field during a kick-off, keeping them at least 10 yards away from the ball.

THROW-IN

TERMS AND DEFINITIONS

RESTART — Putting the ball back into play after a stop in the action. There are 5 types of restarts:

- THROW-IN — A player, standing outside of the touch-line, throws the ball into the field of play using both hands from behind and over his head.

  - A throw-in for a team takes place after an opposing player is the last one to touch the ball before the entire ball crosses over the touch-line (either on the ground or in the air).

  - After the throw-in, the thrower cannot touch the ball until another player touches it.

  - The thrower must be facing the field when he releases the ball. Therefore, a player cannot throw it over his head with his back to the field (which could give his throw more distance).

  - The thrower must have both feet either on the touch-line or on the ground behind the touch-line where the ball passed out-of-bounds.

  - A throw-in that goes directly into a goal does not count as a score. The ball must first be touched by another player.

- GOAL-KICK — The ball is placed anywhere within the goal-area and is kicked by the team defending that area.

  - A goal-kick takes place after a player on the *attacking* team is the last one to touch the ball before the entire ball crosses over the goal-line (except into the goal) either on the ground or in the air.

CORNER-KICK

- Any player on the defending team may kick the ball on a goal-kick.

- The kicked ball must go outside of the penalty-area.

    1. Opposing players may not enter the penalty-area until the ball has left that penalty-area.

    2. A goal-kick that does not go outside of the penalty-area is retaken.

- The kicker may not touch the ball after he kicks it, unless it has touched another player.

- A goal is not scored if a goal-kick goes all the way into the other goal without touching another player.

- CORNER-KICK — The ball is placed in the quarter circle arc at a corner of the field and kicked by the attacking team.

    - A corner-kick takes place after a player on the *defending* team is the last one to touch the ball before the entire ball crosses over the goal-line (except into the goal) either on the ground or in the air. The ball is kicked from the corner of the field closest to where the ball went over the goal-line.

    - After he kicks it, the kicker may not touch the ball until it has touched another player.

    - Opposing players must stand at least 10 yards away from the ball until it has been kicked into play (and the ball has gone at least the distance of its circumference: 27 to 28 inches).

    - If a corner-kick curves into the goal without touching another player, a goal is scored.

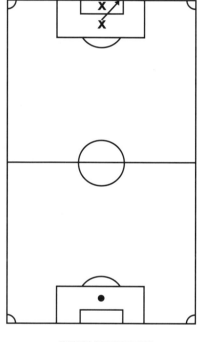

PENALTY-KICK

- FREE-KICK — A kick awarded to a team whose opponent committed a violation.
    - Two types of free-kicks are:
        1. INDIRECT — A kick that must first touch another player before going into the goal. It usually is a result of a *minor* violation (discussed in the Fouls and Misconduct section).
        2. DIRECT — A kick that can go directly into the goal without first touching another player. It usually is a result of a *major* violation (discussed in the Fouls and Misconduct section).
    - After he kicks it, the kicker may not touch the ball until it has touched another player.
    - Opposing players must stand at least 10 yards away from a free-kick until the ball has traveled the distance of its circumference (27 to 28 inches).
    - If a free-kick is taken within one's penalty-area, the kicked ball must go outside of the penalty-area.
        1. Opposing players may not enter the penalty-area until the ball has left that penalty-area.
        2. A free-kick that does not go outside of the penalty-area is retaken.
    - If a free-kick is taken within 10 yards of the opponent's goal, then opposing players may stand on the goal-line between the goal posts.
- PENALTY-KICK — A direct free-kick awarded to the attacking team when a defender commits a major violation in the defending team's penalty-area.
    - The kick takes place from the mark on the field 12 yards from the center of the goal.

TACKLE

- All players (except the kicker and the goal-keeper) must be within the field, outside of the penalty-area, but at least 10 yards behind the spot of the kick. (An arc on the outside of each penalty-area guides the players where to stand.)

- The goalkeeper must stand on the goal-line between the goal posts, without moving his feet, until the ball is kicked.

- The kicker may not touch the ball after he kicks it, unless it has touched another player.

  1. If the penalty-kick bounces off the goal post, the kicker cannot touch the ball until it has been touched by another player.

  2. If the penalty-kick is deflected into the field of play by the goalkeeper, the kicker can kick the ball because it *has* been touched by another player.

- It is estimated that 80–90% of penalty-kicks attempted result in a score.

TACKLE — A defender attempts to take the ball away from an opposing player. Unlike the violent play of the same name in American football, the defender *must* go for the *ball*, not the body, of the opposing player. A cleanly performed tackle can leave the defender with the ball and the opposing player untouched. The purpose is *not*, as in American football, to knock the opposing player to the ground, it is to take away the ball.

- Because players (except the goalkeeper) cannot use their hands, tackling is done by using their feet.

MARKING

DRIBBLING

- If a player slides while trying to take the ball away from the ballcarrier, it is called a SLIDING TACKLE.
  - With a sliding tackle, the defender takes advantage of his outstretched leg when trying to get the ball.
  - The downside risk is that the ballcarrier may avoid the tackle and bypass the defender, who must then get up from the ground.
  - The defender must not make contact with the ballcarrier before making contact with the ball and cannot slide in a way that puts the ballcarrier in danger.

DRIBBLE— A player controls the ball with his feet while moving.

NUTMEG — A player dribbles the ball through an opponent's legs and regains possession on the other side.

FEINTING — An offensive player fakes a move in one direction, causing an opposing player to go in that direction. Frequently, this frees the offensive player to go a different way.

MARKING — A defender stays close to an opposing player to make it difficult for him to pass or receive the ball. In other sports such as basketball, this is similar to "guarding."

JOCKEYING — A defender, in a semi-crouched position, stays near the ballcarrier (but not right on top of him) and does not respond to his feints. The purpose of jockeying is to slow down the ballcarrier without trying to tackle him.

HEADING

SHEPHERDING — A form of jockeying, but the defender turns his body, leading the ballcarrier to move in a certain direction.

CLEARING — A defender moves the ball away from a dangerous situation (usually when the ball is in front of the goal he is defending) as quickly as possible.

SCREENING — The person with possession of the ball puts himself between the defender and the ball, making it difficult for the defender to tackle him.

VOLLEYING — Striking the ball while it is in the air.

SCISSORS KICK — A move where a player jumps and kicks the ball with his foot over his head.
- The crowd loves the acrobatics on a scissors kick, especially if it results in a goal.
- This type of kick cannot be done near an opposing player, as it is considered too dangerous to an opponent.
- Some refer to this type of kick as a BICYCLE KICK.

HEADING — As the ball approaches him, the player strikes it with his forehead.
- This is one of the most thrilling plays in soccer, especially when a player heads a ball into the goal.
- For safety reasons, a player cannot head a ball that is below his chest when a defender is near, so that the player won't get kicked in the head.

CENTER or CROSS — A pass from a side of the field to the center near the goal, with the intent of creating an opportunity for a teammate to score a goal.

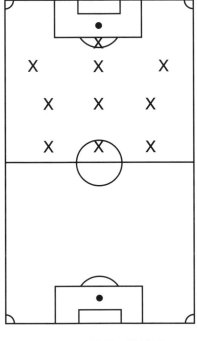

4-3-3 FORMATION

TRAPPING — A player brings the ball under control by using any part of his body except his hands and arms.

SHOOT — A player on the attacking team attempts to score by kicking or heading the ball toward the goal.

GOAL — When the entire ball has passed over the goal-line, between the goal posts and under the crossbar, provided it was not last touched by the hand or arm of a player on the *attacking* team. If the ball is last touched by a *defender*'s hand or arm before entering the goal, it counts as a goal against that defending team.

HAT TRICK — A player scores three goals in a game.

SAVE — A goalkeeper prevents an opponent from scoring by stopping the ball from entering the goal.

FORMATION — The alignment of players on the field. The formation does not include the goalkeeper because his position (in front of the goal) is nearly always the same.

- In describing formations, a count of players is used, starting with the players closest to the goalkeeper.
- For example, a 4-3-3 formation has 4 players (defenders) across the field fairly close to their goal. The next 3 players (midfielders) are farther from their goal, and the last 3 players (forwards) are positioned farthest away from their goal.

WEAK SIDE — The side of the field away from the ball. If the ball is on the left side of the field, the right side is the weak side.

WING AREA — The area of the field closest to each touch-line.

GOALKEEPER

THE PLAYERS ON THE FIELD
(IN A 4-3-3 FORMATION)

GOALKEEPER — The player whose ultimate responsibility is to prevent the opposing team from scoring a goal.

- The goalkeeper has the unique privilege of using his hands or arms to catch or deflect a ball while he is in the penalty-area.

- The goalkeeper wears a different-colored shirt than his teammates, so he will stand out from the other players.

- Because the goalkeeper is the only player always facing the action, he frequently directs his teammates on defense.

- The goalkeeper is usually tall, which helps him cover the wide area of the GOAL (between the goal posts and under the crossbar).

- The goalkeeper usually has good catching skills, reflexes, jumping ability, courage and intelligence.

- The goalkeeper prefers to catch or "keep" the ball instead of merely deflecting it in front of the goal where it might create the opportunity for another shot by an opponent.

- When catching the ball, the goalkeeper softens the impact by CUSHIONING with his hands (moving them in the direction the ball is traveling) while attempting to catch the ball, as if he were catching an egg tossed at him.

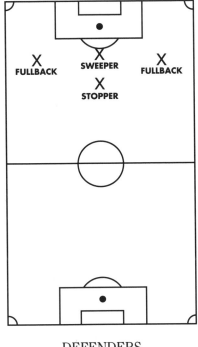

DEFENDERS

FULLBACKS (left and right) — Players positioned to the left and right of the goal they are defending. Their primary responsibility is to fend off attacks from the sides of the field.

- A fullback moves up the field with his team, when it has the ball, to be in a position to assist with the attack or to return any balls that may be cleared by the opposing team.

- Fullbacks must work together. If one of them comes to the outside to mark an attacker with the ball, the other fullback must move to the center to protect against a CENTER PASS.

- They must be quick, to keep up with attackers from the outside.

- Most are skilled dribblers and passers, as they initiate plays after gaining possession of the ball.

- Fullbacks usually have the ability to jump, in order to head the ball out of the danger areas in front of the goal.

SWEEPER — Player positioned near the goal in the center of the field. Basically, he is a center fullback.

- His main purpose is to "sweep" away a ball coming to the goal before it can even reach the goalkeeper.

- He has no marking responsibility except to stay close to an offensive player who "breaks through" the defense.

STOPPER or MARKING BACK — A fullback-type player positioned in front of the sweeper.

- His main responsibility is to break up any attacks in the center of the field before they get dangerously close to the goal.

- He will frequently mark the opposing team's center forward (discussed below).

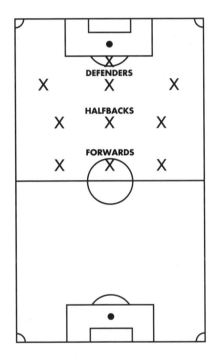

- Many times, he gains possession of the ball as a result of "stopping" the attack, and he then starts the counterattack.

HALFBACKS or MIDFIELDERS (left, center and right) — Positioned ahead of the fullbacks, participating on defense and often initiating the offensive attack.

- They are the most versatile players on the field because of their dual roles.
- The halfbacks on a team usually mark the halfbacks on the opposing team.
- They are aggressive tacklers, especially in the midfield area.
- Many games are decided by which team's halfbacks "control" the midfield area.

FORWARDS, STRIKERS or ATTACKERS (left, center and right) — Players who make up the front line of attack with an emphasis on scoring goals.

- The center forward is closest to the opponent's goal, so he is usually the leading scorer on the team. Two of the most famous center forwards, past and present, are Brazil's *Pelé* and Argentina's *Maradona*.
- Forwards are able to dribble at top speed and are skilled at shooting (to score goals), passing (for centering) and jumping (for heading).
- While their team is defending, some forwards stay near the halfway-line, so in case their team regains possession of the ball, they'll have a head start to the opponent's goal.

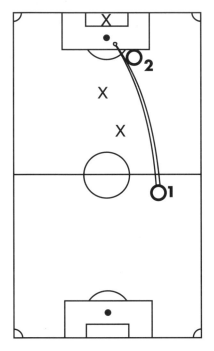

Player 2 is off-side when player 1 takes a shot because there are not at least two defending players between him and the goal. He is also on the opponent's side of the field and potentially involved in the play: He is "loitering" and called off-side.

OFF-SIDE

The purpose of the off-side rule is to prevent players from "loitering" near the goal, waiting for a pass from a teammate.

A player is off-side if he is closer to the opponent's goal-line than the ball is, when the ball is touched by a teammate.

A player is *not* ruled off-side if:

- He is on his team's half of the field.
- He is not nearer to the goal than at least two opposing players (the goalkeeper counts as one opposing player).
- He receives the ball directly from a goal-kick, corner-kick or throw-in.
- At the moment the ball touches a teammate, the player is not trying to gain an advantage.
- At the moment the ball touches a teammate, the player is not "interfering" with play or an opponent.
- He was not in an off-side position at the time the ball was passed to him from a teammate, but is in an off-side position at the time he receives it.

When a player is ruled off-side, the opposing team is awarded an indirect free-kick at the point where the player was called off-side.

Excessively rough play is not allowed in soccer. Player 1 is guilty of a major violation by pushing player 2. The result is a direct free-kick for player 2's team.

FOULS AND MISCONDUCT

A DIRECT FREE-KICK is awarded to a team's opponent when a team *intentionally* commits one of the following major violations:

- KICKS or attempts to kick an opponent.

- TRIPS an opponent.

- JUMPS at an opponent.

- CHARGES an opponent violently or in a dangerous manner.

- CHARGES an opponent from behind, unless the opponent is obstructing (see "OBSTRUCTION" below).

- STRIKES or spits at an opponent.

- HOLDS an opponent.

- PUSHES an opponent.

- HANDLES the ball with his hands or arms (except the goalkeeper in his penalty area).

A PENALTY-KICK is awarded to a team's opponent if one of the above violations is intentionally committed by a team within its own penalty-area.

An INDIRECT FREE-KICK is awarded to a team's opponent when a team commits the following violations:

- Dangerous play that puts a player or his opponent at risk.

  - Attempting to kick the ball that is held by the goalkeeper.

  - Kicking near an opponent's head.

  - Heading a ball below one's chest near an opponent.

- Charging an opponent when the ball is not within 3 feet of the players.

OBSTRUCTION

Player 1 is not going for
the ball and is interfering
with player 2. Player 1 is
guilty of obstruction, and
an indirect free-kick is
awarded to player 2's team.

- OBSTRUCTION — Intentionally blocking an opponent from getting to the ball instead of going after the ball.

- Charging the goalkeeper, except when he is outside the goal-area.

- Within his penalty-area, a goalkeeper takes more than 4 steps while controlling the ball with his hands, either by holding or bouncing it.

- After releasing the ball, the goalkeeper touches it before it has been touched by a teammate outside of the penalty-area or by a player of the opposing team either inside or outside of the penalty-area.

- The goalkeeper touches the ball with his hands after it is deliberately kicked to him by a teammate.

- When a goalkeeper purposefully does anything that wastes time.

A player receives a CAUTION (and is shown a symbolic YELLOW CARD by the referee) if he:

- Enters or leaves the field without receiving permission from an official.

- Continues to break the rules.

- Shows disagreement with an official's call, either verbally or by gestures.

- Is guilty of ungentlemanly conduct such as purposely delaying the game, or boosting himself up to head the ball by using a teammate's shoulders.

A player will be EJECTED (and shown a symbolic RED CARD), removed from the game and declared ineligible for the team's next game if he:

- Is guilty of violent conduct or serious foul play.

- Uses foul and abusive language.

- Receives a second caution.

REFEREE

OFFICIALS

REFEREE — He is the one in charge. There's only one referee per game.

- He enforces the rules.
  - The referee abides by the ADVANTAGE RULE (which he expresses by calling out, "Play on, advantage."). This means that he should not call a penalty which would benefit the *offending* team. For example, if an opponent charges into the ballcarrier from behind, but the ballcarrier did not lose his balance and continued toward the goal, the referee should not call the foul.
  - Before a referee calls a foul, he pauses a second to determine if a foul called would harm the offended team.
- He serves as the timekeeper, including adding to the regulation time any time lost to injuries, time-wasting or substitutions.
- Shows a YELLOW CARD to any player receiving a caution.
- Shows a RED CARD to any player who is ejected.
  - If a player receives a second yellow card, he is also shown a red card to signify that he was ejected for 2 cautions.
  - The ejected player cannot be replaced, so a team plays one player short. (The team does not have to play a player short in the next game, even though the ejected player is ineligible to play.)

SUBSTITUTION SIGNAL

Two LINESMEN assist the referee.

- They indicate when the ball is out of play.

- They indicate which team is entitled to a goal-kick, corner-kick or throw-in.

- They indicate when a team wants to make a substitution.

- They indicate when a player is in an off-side position.

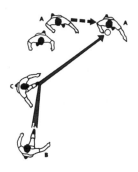

TRIANGLE OF THREE OFFENSIVE PLAYERS

COMMON OFFENSIVE STRATEGIES

In order to score a goal, the offense strives to accomplish the following:

- Maintain possession of the ball through passing, dribbling and heading.

- Move toward the goal (with or without the ball) by avoiding defenders using feints, speed and adept dribbling.

- Spread out the defense by using the entire width of the field and not bunching up. This tactic helps a team create holes (open spaces) in the defense— through which passes can be made, or offensive dribbling "strikes" towards the goal can be made.

- Create "TRIANGLES" with the person who has possession of the ball. There are two types of triangles.

  - An offensive player positions himself so that a triangle is created with the ballcarrier and a defender marking the ballcarrier. In this case, the offense avoids allowing an opponent to get between the person with the ball and a teammate without it. Otherwise, it would be easy for the defender to steal the pass made between the offensive players.

  - Two offensive players position themselves so that a triangle is created with the ballcarrier. In this case, the defenders do not know to which player the ball will be passed.

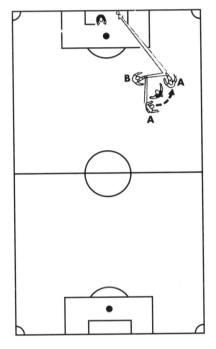

WALL PASS

Offensive player A passes to offensive player B, and player A quickly moves around defender to receive ball passed from player B, as if it had bounced off of a wall.

Techniques a team can use to achieve the above objectives:

- WALL PASS or GIVE AND GO — A player receives a pass from a teammate and immediately deflects it back to him as if it had bounced off a "wall."

  - The defender marking the teammate relaxes a bit when he sees the person he is marking give up the ball.

  - To capitalize on the defender's relaxation, the teammate runs by him and retrieves the wall pass.

- TAKEOVER — The player with the ball moves in one direction and leaves it for a teammate behind him moving in the opposite direction. This tactic frequently confuses the defensive team because of the quick change in direction.

- THROUGH PASS — A pass through the defense to an attacking teammate running toward the goal.

  - Timing is important so that the receiver of the pass is not off-side when the ball is passed to him.

  - Sometimes this pass is referred to as a PENETRATING PASS, because it is used to "penetrate" the open spaces in the defense.

- WEAK-SIDE PASS or DIAGONAL PASS — A pass from one side of the field to the other, used when the defense has focused primarily on the side of the field where the ball is being played (leaving the other side or the "weak-side" of the field open for attack).

- LONG PUNT — After a goalkeeper picks up the ball in the penalty-area, he kicks it downfield aiming for his tall teammates so they can head the ball to another teammate. The purpose of this kick is to put the ball in the opponent's side of the field in a teammate's possession.

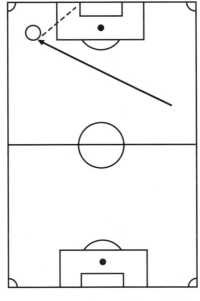

CROSS TO THE FAR POST

- CROSS TO THE FAR POST — A pass across the goal-area to a teammate which could result in that teammate heading the ball for a goal, or the teammate heading it to a colleague standing close to the near post. This change of direction can confuse the defense and lead to a goal.

- OVERLAPPING FULLBACK — In order to outnumber the defense, an attacking team may allow its fullback to overlap (bypass) the opposing team's forward to join the attack.

- TEASING — The ballcarrier offers the ball to a defender by rolling it to him (with his foot), but then stops it with the sole of his foot. This tactic enables the offensive player to bypass the defender who has committed to go in one direction.

- CHIP SHOT — A lofted shot over any defender, including the goalkeeper who has come out of the goal-area. (This is very similar to the lob shot in tennis). A chip shot over the goalkeeper could go into the goal and make him think twice about leaving the goal-area next time, giving the attacking team better angles to the goal.

When the ball goes over the touch-line or goal-line, teams may have a strategy on the restart. The following are strategies used when putting the ball back into play.

- On a throw-in:
    - Usually, the person who is closest to where the ball crossed the touch-line is responsible for the throw-in, leaving the defense with little time to set up for the play.

    - Some teams may have a specialist who can throw the ball a long way.

    - A player may throw the ball toward his own goal to the goalkeeper, who may pick it up if he is in the penalty-area.

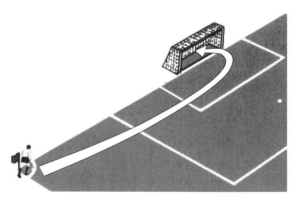

INSWERVING KICK
ON A CORNER KICK

In a real game there would
be players and a goalie
involved in the play.

- If near the opponent's goal, a player may throw the ball in the vicinity of the goal area so that a teammate may head it in.

- A wall-pass could confuse the defense, as the thrower is often ignored.

- Remember that off-side is not called on a player who receives a pass directly from a throw-in.

- On a corner-kick:

  - The conventional method is to kick the ball across the penalty-area at "head height" so a teammate may attempt to head it into the goal.

    1. An "outswerving kick" or "outswinger" curves away from the goal and is ideal for a teammate's head shot.

    2. An "inswerving kick" or "inswinger" curves toward the goal and is used to challenge an inept goalkeeper.

  - The short-kick method involves kicking the ball to a teammate who is close by.

    1. A short-kick is used when conditions are windy or the team does not have a strong kicker or a strong header.

    2. A short-kick draws the defense out of the goal-area, creating open spaces.

  - Remember that off-side is not called on a player who receives the ball directly from a corner-kick.

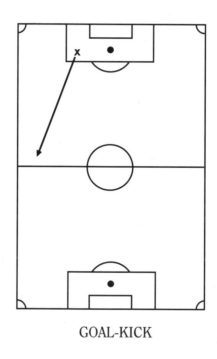

GOAL-KICK

- On a goal-kick:
    - The ball should be kicked away from the middle of the field, in case possession of the ball is lost.
    - A goal-kick is usually kicked by the goalkeeper or a fullback so that the halfbacks and forwards can immediately start "attacking."

Verbal signals are used between teammates to inform each other of happenings on the field. Some of these signals include:

- SQUARE — The player who yells this signal is either at or about to come up to a position even with the ballcarrier.

- BACK — The player who yells this signal is informing the ballcarrier that he is behind him.

- MAN ON — This signal tells a player that a defender, who is currently out of his sight, will soon be marking him.

- TIME — This signal tells the ballcarrier that a defender is not near him and he has time to make a play.

When a team is losing by a goal late in the game, there are a couple of "extra" offensive actions that it might decide to employ.

- Substitute a forward (attacker) into the game in place of a fullback, switching from the common 4-3-3 formation to a 3-3-4 formation.

- Bring the goalkeeper to the halfway-line when his team is on attack, to have him participate in a scoring opportunity.

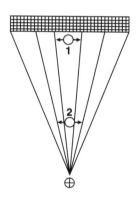

NARROWING THE ANGLE

The scoring angle is reduced by the goalkeeper moving from position 1 to position 2.

COMMON DEFENSIVE STRATEGIES

Methods used by the defense to make it difficult for the opponents to score are as follows:

- After losing possession of the ball, to give fellow teammates time to set up defensively, the player closest to the ball should immediately jockey the ballcarrier to slow him down.

- The defensive players should crowd the penalty-area, making it difficult for the opposing players or the ball to penetrate.

- Defensive players should "support" each other by running to fill any holes on defense that may have been created by teammates who went to challenge the ballcarrier.

- Defenders need to avoid responding to offensive feints, so they will not be out of position.

- Defenders attempt to force the offensive players to travel in undesired routes such as close to the touch-lines.

- Tackle an opponent, taking the ball away.

- Intercept a pass from the attacking team.

- Narrow the Angle — Usually applies to when the goalkeeper advances toward a player who has possession of the ball. As the goalkeeper approaches the ballcarrier, the margin of a potential scoring kick (that will get between the goalkeeper and one of the goal posts) is geometrically reduced. To illustrate, form a triangle (with the goal-line as the base) by drawing a line from a ballcarrier to each goal post. Put the goalkeeper on the goal-line. From the ballcarrier's perspective, note the substantial amount of space ("wide angles") between the goalkeeper and each goal post. As the goalkeeper (with outstretched arms) comes closer to the ballcarrier, these spaces become smaller,

CHIP SHOT

thus narrowing the angle of the ballcarrier's scoring opportunities. This strategy can, however, be risky. With the goalkeeper out of position, the defending team is vulnerable to:

- The ballcarrier's passing the ball to a teammate.

- The ballcarrier's dribbling around the goalkeeper.

- The ballcarrier's lifting the ball over the goalkeeper's head using a CHIP SHOT.

- SHOULDER CHARGE — Using shoulder to shoulder contact, a defender pushes an opponent away from the ball.

  - This is one of the few forms of physical contact that is allowed in soccer.

  - A shoulder charge cannot take place from behind the offensive player.

  - A shoulder charge may not be done in a violent or dangerous manner.

  - A shoulder charge must take place within playing distance (3 feet) of the ball and the players must be attempting to get to the ball, not just knocking a player out of the way.

- Defensive players mark specific offensive players—especially the best shooters and passers—to prevent them from receiving or passing the ball, limiting the offense's choice of strategies.

- ZONE COVERAGE — Instead of marking a specific offensive player, a defender is assigned to a zone or area in the field.

  - This type of defense is sometimes called ZONAL MARKING.

  - If a certain zone is FLOODED with offensive players, other defenders must come to their teammate's aid.

JOCKEYING

- If a ballcarrier is running past a defender, the defender tries to ensure that the ballcarrier passes him on the side closest to the touch-line. This delays the time it takes the ballcarrier to get closer to the goal.

- JOCKEYING — Marking an opponent from a few steps away, attempting to force him to move in a certain direction (shepherding). The reasons for this defensive tactic are:

  - Some players are poor left-footed kickers. If a defender can shepherd a poor left-footed ballcarrier to the left wing area, it is difficult for the ballcarrier to kick the ball to the center of the field. He will either have to use his weaker left foot or the outside of his right foot.

  - A defender may shepherd a ballcarrier to an area occupied by a teammate of the defender. Two defenders marking one ballcarrier frequently results in a successful tackle.

- OFF-SIDE TRAP — A defender moves upfield past an opponent to put that player in an off-side position. The risk of an official not making the call is a factor in considering this strategy.

- Some teams may choose a formation using only one or two strikers to put more emphasis on defense.

Defensively, teams may have a strategy on a restart:

- On a throw-in:

  - In an effort to intercept the ball, each member of the defense will mark an offensive player on a throw-in.

  - The defense cannot afford to ignore the thrower because of the possibility of a wall pass.

WALL OF DEFENDERS

- If a throw-in is close to the thrower's penalty-area, a defender will mark the goalkeeper. This tactic minimizes the opportunity of the goalkeeper's picking up the throw-in and punting the ball downfield.

- On a corner-kick:

  - A fullback normally will be placed at the goal posts on each side of the goalkeeper. This allows the goalkeeper to leave the goal-area to save a corner-kick or a subsequent kick by another player.

  - Each fullback plays the role of a goalkeeper who cannot use his hands.

- On a free-kick (within shooting distance of the goal):

  - A WALL of defenders, standing shoulder to shoulder, is formed to block the path of the ball.

  - The goalkeeper positions his defensive teammates in front of the most direct path of the ball to the goal. He then covers the remainder of the exposed goal.

  - The defense should be prepared for a chip shot over the wall.

  - The defense should also focus on players other than the kicker, as they might receive a pass around the wall for a clear shot at the goal. Some attackers might stand in front of the wall and move just as the ball is being kicked, distracting these defensive players.

The United States, host of the 1994 World Cup championship tournament in the summer of '94 (see appendices for dates and cities), has competed in the final round of 24 teams only four times: in 1930, 1934, 1950 and in 1990. The U.S. team, which earned its way to the 1990 tournament, automatically qualified for the 1994 World Cup because of its status as the host team.

THE WORLD CUP CHAMPIONSHIP

The world championship of professional soccer.

It began in 1930 and continued every 4 years, except for a 12-year hiatus (1938-1950) during World War II and the post-war years.

The World Cup was created because the Olympics only allowed amateurs.

- Professionals wanted to showcase their talents while representing their countries.

- Now, the Olympics allows professionals. However, most team members must be under 24 years old. Each team is allowed no more than 3 players 24 years old or older.

- The women's teams have no age restrictions.

Nearly 150 teams play in a series of matches during the 2 years prior to the World Cup. Only 22 teams qualify from this process.

The host country and the defending champion automatically complete the field of 24 for the World Cup.

The first round of the World Cup consists of teams divided into 6 groups of 4, with each team playing the other 3 in its group.

- FIFA, the governing body of the World Cup, picks the 6 strongest teams and puts each of them in separate groups.

- The remaining 3 teams in each group are determined by draw. Some precautions are taken so that not too many teams from the same region of the world are in the same group.

Of approximately 150 teams which compete for their country across the globe in preliminary games to qualify for the World Cup championship tournament, only five nations have emerged in the final tournament as multiple winners: Brazil, Italy and West Germany (3); and Argentina and Uruguay (2). England, another perennial soccer power, has won only once, in 1966.

After the first round, the top 2 teams in each group and the 4 best third-place teams advance to the second round (the final 16) as determined by total points (3 points for a win and 1 for a tie).

The second round consists of 8 games between the final 16 teams. The winners advance to the next round, while the losers are eliminated. Then, 2 more rounds are played until the final 2 teams meet in the championship game. There cannot be a tie or draw.

- If there is a tie in the score after regulation play, 2 additional 15 minute periods are played. Whichever team scores more goals during the extra 30 minutes of play wins. If it is still tied, the teams have a series of penalty-kicks.

    - All kicks are directed at one goal as designated by the referee.

    - The referee tosses a coin, and the winner goes first.

    - Each team takes 5 penalty-kicks, alternating between each team. If more than 5 are needed to determine a winner, each takes one more kick until it makes a goal while the other does not.

    - Each kick is taken by a different player who was on the field when regulation play ended (including the goalkeepers).

    - Only the kicker and the two goalkeepers can be outside of the center circle during the penalty-kicks. The goalkeeper who is a teammate of the kicker must be at least 10 yards away from the kicker.

The passion that each country's fans have for their World Cup team is unparalleled. The broadcasters display this emotion when a goal is scored, shouting, "GOGOGOGOGOGOGOGOOGOGOGOGOGOGOGOGOGOAL" or "GOOOOOOOOOOOOOOOOOOOOOOOOOOOOOOOAL."

INDEX

SOCCER QUIZ #1

1. If a penalty-kick attempt strikes a goal post and comes back to the kicker who then heads it into the goal past the goalkeeper. *What is the result?*

    a. Two goals.
    b. One goal.
    c. No goal.
    d. Retry the penalty-kick.

2. *Which player is most likely to be the leading scorer on a soccer team?*

    a. Stopper.
    b. Left fullback.
    c. Sweeper.
    d. Center forward.

3. As a player kicks the ball to a teammate on a corner-kick, this teammate is standing in front of the goal with only the goalkeeper in between. The teammate volleys the ball into the goal with his foot. *What is the result?*

    a. Goal-kick.
    b. Off-side
    c. Goal
    d. Another corner-kick.

4. As a player dribbles up the left side of the field, he sees his teammate all alone near the right corner flag (with no one between that teammate and the goal-line). The player feints his defender out of the play and kicks the ball into the goal. *What is the result?*

    a. Goal-kick.
    b. Off-side.
    c. Goal.
    d. Corner-kick.

SOCCER QUIZ #1 (CONT'D)

5. A team is losing by one point with a minute left in the game. The fullback dribbles the ball in his penalty-area and then kicks it to his goalkeeper, who picks up the ball. After taking a couple of steps, the goalkeeper punts the ball past the halfway-line to a teammate who kicks the ball into the goal. *What is the result?*

    a. Indirect free-kick.
    b. Goal.
    c. Penalty-kick.
    d. Corner-kick.

6. An attacker dribbles the ball near the left corner of the field and the ball barely touches the goal-line. He then centers the ball to a teammate who heads it into the goal. *What is the result?*

    a. Goal-kick.
    b. Corner-kick.
    c. Goal.
    d. Throw-in.

7. A player heads the ball toward the goal, and it crosses the goal-line between the goal posts and under the crosssbar. However, before the ball hits the net, the goalkeeper punches the ball to a teammate who clears it over the goal-line. *What is the result?*

    a. Goal-kick.
    b. Corner-kick.
    c. Goal.
    d. Throw-in.

8. An attacker kicks the ball toward the goal, but the goalkeeper deflects the ball over the crossbar. *What is the result?*

    a. Goal-kick.
    b. Corner-kick.
    c. Goal.
    d. Throw-in.

9. A player is cautioned with his second yellow card of the game for arguing with the referee. *What is the result?*

    a. The player also receives a red card and is ejected from the game.
    b. The player's team must finish the game with one less player on the field.
    c. The ejected player may not play in the team's next game.
    d. All of the above.

10. A player inadvertently kicks the ball toward the touch-line. The ball passes over the line in the air and as it is about to hit the ground behind the line, a teammate kicks the ball back into play. The ball is then kicked into the goal. *What is the result?*

    a. Goal-kick.
    b. Corner-kick.
    c. Goal.
    d. Throw-in.

ANSWERS TO SOCCER QUIZ #1

1. (c) A goal is not scored because a kicker of a free-kick (including a penalty-kick) cannot touch the ball after he kicks it, unless the ball touches another player. Because the kicker touched the ball first, the opposing team is awarded an indirect free-kick.

2. (d) The center forward position is closest to the opponent's goal, so a coach ensures that his top scorer plays that position.

3. (c) A goal is scored. Off-side is not called on a player who directly receives a corner-kick.

4. (c) A goal is scored. A player is not necessarily ruled off-side merely because he is in an off-side position. He must "interfere with an opponent or the play, or be seeking to gain an advantage" to be ruled off-side. If the scoring player's teammate was in an off-side position and was not a factor in the play (as determined by the referee), he should not be ruled off-side.

5. (a) An indirect free-kick is awarded where the goalkeeper touched the ball. When a player intentionally kicks the ball to his own goalkeeper, the goalkeeper is not allowed to touch the ball with his hands. This rule was enacted to speed up the game. Previously, many teams ahead in the score would frequently kick the ball to their own goalkeeper to waste time at the expense of their opponents and spectators.

6. (c) A goal is scored. The goal-lines and touch-lines are in the field of play, so unless the entire ball crosses outside the line, play continues.

7. (c) A goal is scored once the entire ball crosses the goal-line between the goal posts and under the crossbar. The net only stops the ball after a goal is scored and has no other significance.

8. (b) The attacking team is awarded a corner-kick when the ball passes over the goal-line (except between the goal posts and under the crossbar) and a member of the defending team is the last one to touch it. If the attacking team was the last to touch the ball before it went over the goal-line, the defending team would be awarded a goal-kick.

9. (d) All of the above. After a player receives a second yellow card he immediately receives a red card indicating that he is ejected from the current game and the team's next game. His team plays with one less player on the field during the current game (but in the next game, he can be replaced so that his team can play with 11 players on the field).

10. (d) If a team member causes the ball to completely pass over the touch-line, play stops and a throw-in by the opponents is the restart. It is not relevant that the ball never touched the ground beyond the touch-line.

SOCCER QUIZ #2

Pretend you are in the following situations:

1. The team that you coach just gave up the tie break-ing goal with about two minutes left in the game. Currently, your team is in a 4-3-3 formation. *What might you do?*

    a. Call time-out.
    b. Replace one of your fullbacks or other defenders with a forward.
    c. Replace your center forward with a fullback.
    d. Replace one of your midfielders with anoth-er sweeper.

2. The opposing team's goalkeeper constantly comes out of the goal-area to narrow the angle on your team's attackers, leaving the goal somewhat unpro-tected. *What might you do if you were the ballcar-rier in the opposing team's penalty-area?*

    a. Chip shot over the goalkeeper.
    b. Pass the ball to a teammate in an off-side position.
    c. Shoulder charge the goalkeeper.
    d. Tackle the sweeper.

3. Your goalkeeper just made a diving save of a shot toward the goal. The ball rebounded to you, the sweeper, just in front of the goal. *What might you do?*

    a. Kick the ball to your goalkeeper.
    b. Clear the ball out of the goal-area.
    c. Nutmeg through the closest opponent.
    d. Tackle the opposing center forward.

SOCCER QUIZ #2 (CONT'D)

4. You are dribbling the ball on the left side of the field and are about to be surrounded by two opponents. On the right side of the field is an unmarked teammate. *What might you do?*

    a. Shoulder charge through both opponents.
    b. Wait for a teammate to obstruct one of the opposing players.
    c. Trap the ball with your arms.
    d. Weak-side pass.

5. You are about to take a corner-kick. One of your tall forwards is on the opposite side of the goal-area, ready for a header. *What might you do?*

    a. Weak-side pass.
    b. Takeover.
    c. Cross to the far post.
    d. Short kick.

6. The opposing team has been awarded a direct free-kick just outside of your penalty area. *What should you do defensively?*

    a. If you are a fullback, you should overlap a forward.
    b. Mark the opposing team's goalkeeper.
    c. Set up a wall in the direct path from the ball to the goal.
    d. Stand next to the kicker.

7. A forward is dribbling the ball on the right side of the field. You are marking him. *What might you do?*

    a. Shepherd him toward the touch-line.
    b. Shoulder charge him from behind.
    c. Shepherd him toward your goalkeeper.
    d. Feint him toward the touch-line.

SOCCER QUIZ #2 (CONT'D)

8. You are the sweeper, and you notice that only the goalkeeper is behind you. The ball is near the center circle controlled by the opposing team. An opposing forward is just ahead of you on the right side of the field. *What might you do defensively?*

    a. Run behind the goalkeeper to cause an off-side trap.

    b. Charge the opposing forward.

    c. Move up the field, passing the opposing forward to cause an offside trap.

    d. Tackle the opposing forward.

9. You are near the touch-line on a throw-in. Your teammate is the thrower, and you notice that he is not being marked. *What might your strategy be on the throw-in?*

    a. Kick it back to the thrower.

    b. Sliding tackle.

    c. Obstructing a defender.

    d. Hat trick.

10. Your team has a pass intercepted in the opponent's penalty-area. *What should your team do immediately to prepare for the counterattack?*

    a. Mark the opposing team's goalkeeper so he can't receive the ball for a long punt.

    b. Your teammate closest to the ballcarrier should jockey that opposing player.

    c. Set up a wall at the halfway-line to prevent penetration into your side of the field.

    d. Your goalkeeper should come out of the goal-area to narrow the angle of attack.

ANSWERS TO SOCCER QUIZ #2

1. (b) Change to a 3-3-4 formation by adding an extra forward and removing one of your fullbacks. When a team is losing late in the game, it is advisable to risk some defense for a better opportunity to score.

2. (a) A chip shot over the goalkeeper could go into the goal and influence the goalkeeper to stay in the goal-area next time, giving your team better angles to the goal in the future.

3. (b) A defender who finds the ball in front of his goal should instinctively clear it out of that area to eliminate a scoring possibility.

4. (d) A weak-side pass is an excellent technique to avoid an overcrowded defense on one side of the field. Better opportunities to attack and score might be available on the other side.

5. (c) A cross pass at "head height" would give your onrushing teammate an ideal opportunity to head the ball into the goal or head the ball to another teammate who might be open for a shot.

6. (c) Set up a wall of defenders to block the ball from directly being kicked into the goal. Your goalkeeper must cover the exposed area of the goal when the ball is kicked.

7. (a) Consider the touch-line as another teammate and try to lead the ballcarrier to this "teammate." Shepherding the opponent to the touch-line will limit his passing and dribbling options.

8. (c) Moving past the forward so that only your goal-keeper is between the opposing player and your goal-line can suppress the opposing team's attack by creating a likely off-sides situation.

9. (a) Returning the pass to an unmarked thrower will give him some dribbling and passing opportunities that could lead to a goal.

10. (b) The objective is to slow down the attack after the interception so that your players can set up defensively. Jockeying the ballcarrier will slow his advancement.

BIBLIOGRAPHY

Cook, Ted. *The Spectator's Guide to Soccer.*
  Soccer Publishing, 1990.

FIFA. *Laws of the Game.*
  Fédération Internationale de Football
  Association, 1993.

French, Liz. *How to Play SOCCER: A Step-By-Step Guide.*
  Jarrold Publishing, 1991.

Harris, Paul. *Spalding Soccer Handbook.*
  Masters Press, 1992.

Miller, Lowell. *Mastering Soccer.*
  Contemporary Books, 1979.

Paul, Nic. *Tactics of Success: Soccer.*
  Ward Lock, 1992.

Rosenthal, Gary. *Everybody's Soccer Book.*
  Charles Scribner's Sons, 1981.

APPENDICES

WORLD CUP

1994 WORLD CUP SCHEDULE

DATES	CITY	VENUE
JUNE 17, 21, 26, 27, JULY 2	CHICAGO	SOLDIER FIELD
JUNE 17, 21, 27, 30, JULY 3	DALLAS	COTTON BOWL
JUNE 18, 22, 24, 28	DETROIT	PONTIAC SILVERDOME
JUNE 18, 19, 22, 26, JULY 3	LOS ANGELES	ROSE BOWL
JUNE 18, 23, 25, 28, JULY 5	NEW YORK/NEW JERSEY	GIANTS STADIUM
JUNE 19, 20, 28, 29, JULY 2	WASHINGTON, D.C.	RFK STADIUM
JUNE 19, 24, 25, 29, JULY 4	ORLANDO	CITRUS BOWL
JUNE 20, 24, 26, 28, JULY 4	SAN FRANCISCO	STANFORD STADIUM
JUNE 21, 23, 25, 30, JULY 5	BOSTON	FOXBORO STADIUM

WORLD CUP FINALS

YEAR	WINNER	RUNNER-UP	SITE
1930	URUGUAY (4)	ARGENTINA (2)	URUGUAY
1934	ITALY (2)	CZECHOSLOVAKIA (1)	ITALY
1938	ITALY (4)	HUNGARY (2)	FRANCE
1950	URUGUAY (2)	BRAZIL (1)	BRAZIL
1954	WEST GERMANY (3)	HUNGARY (2)	SWITZERLAND
1958	BRAZIL (5)	SWEDEN (2)	SWEDEN
1962	BRAZIL (3)	CZECHOSLOVAKIA (1)	CHILE
1966	ENGLAND (4)	WEST GERMANY (2)	ENGLAND
1970	BRAZIL (4)	ITALY (1)	MEXICO
1974	WEST GERMANY (2)	NETHERLANDS (1)	WEST GERMANY
1978	ARGENTINA (3)	NETHERLANDS (1)	ARGENTINA
1982	ITALY (3)	WEST GERMANY (1)	SPAIN
1986	ARGENTINA (3)	WEST GERMANY (2)	MEXICO
1990	WEST GERMANY (1)	ARGENTINA (0)	ITALY

No competition was held in 1942 or 1946 because of World War II.

WORLD CUP GOAL SCORING

YEAR	GAMES	GOALS	AVERAGE	LEADING GOALSCORER	GOALS
1930	18	70	3.88	GUILLERMO STABILE (ARGENTINA)	8
1934	17	70	4.11	ANGELO SCHIAVIO (ITALY)	8
				OLDRICH NEJEDLY (CZECHOSLOVAKIA)	8
				EDMUND COHEN (GERMANY)	4
1938	18	84	4.66	LEONIDAS DA SILVA (BRAZIL)	8
1950	22	88	4.00	ADEMIR (BRAZIL)	9
1954	26	140	5.38	SANDOR KOCSIS (HUNGARY)	11
1958	35	126	3.60	JUST FONTAINE (FRANCE)	13
1962	32	89	2.78	DRAZEN JERKOVIC (YUGOSLAVIA)	5
1966	32	89	2.78	EUSEBIO (PORTUGAL)	9
1970	32	95	2.96	GERD MULLER (WEST GERMANY)	10
1974	38	97	2.55	GRZEGORZ LATO (POLAND)	7
1978	38	102	2.68	MARIO KEMPES (ARGENTINA)	6
1982	52	146	2.81	PAOLO ROSSI (ITALY)	6
1986	52	132	2.53	GARY LINEKER (ENGLAND)	6
1990	52	115	2.21	SALVATORE SCHILLACI (ITALY)	6

WORLD CUP ATTENDANCE

YEAR	SITE	GAMES	TOTAL ATTENDANCE	AVERAGE ATTENDANCE	FINAL VENUE	ATTENDANCE
1930	URUGUAY	18	434,500	24,139	MONTEVIDEO	90,000
1934	ITALY	17	395,000	23,235	ROME	50,000
1938	FRANCE	18	483,000	26,833	PARIS	45,000
1950	BRAZIL	22	1,337,000	60,772	RIO DE JANEIRO	199,854
1954	SWITZERLAND	26	943,000	36,270	BERNE	60,000
1958	SWEDEN	35	868,000	24,800	STOCKHOLM	49,737
1962	CHILE	32	776,000	24,250	SANTIAGO	68,679
1966	ENGLAND	32	1,614,677	50,458	WEMBLEY	93,802
1970	MEXICO	32	1,673,975	52,312	MEXICO CITY	107,412
1974	WEST GERMANY	38	1,774,022	46,685	MUNICH	77,833
1978	ARGENTINA	38	1,610,215	42,374	BUENOS AIRES	77,000
1982	SPAIN	52	1,766,277	33,967	MADRID	90,080
1986	MEXICO	52	2,401,480	46,182	MEXICO CITY	114,580
1990	ITALY	52	2,510,686	48,282	ROME	73,603

OLYMPIC MEDAL WINNERS

	GOLD	SILVER	BRONZE
1900	GREAT BRITAIN	FRANCE	BELGIUM
1904	CANADA	USA I	USA II
1906	DENMARK	SMYRNA (INTL' ENTRY)	GREECE
1908	GREAT BRITAIN	DENMARK	NETHERLANDS
1912	GREAT BRITAIN	DENMARK	NETHERLANDS
1920	BELGIUM	SPAIN	NETHERLANDS
1924	URUGUAY	SWITZERLAND	SWEDEN
1928	URUGUAY	ARGENTINA	ITALY
1936	ITALY	AUSTRIA	NORWAY
1948	SWEDEN	YUGOSLAVIA	DENMARK
1952	HUNGARY	YUGOSLAVIA	SWEDEN
1956	USSR	YUGOSLAVIA	BULGARIA
1960	YUGOSLAVIA	DENMARK	ITALY
1964	HUNGARY	CZECHOSLOVAKIA	GERMANY
1968	HUNGARY	BULGARIA	JAPAN
1972	POLAND	HUNGARY	USSR, EAST GERMANY
1976	EAST GERMANY	POLAND	USSR
1980	CZECHOSLOVAKIA	EAST GERMANY	USSR
1984	FRANCE	BRAZIL	YUGOSLAVIA
1988	USSR	BRAZIL	WEST GERMANY
1992	SPAIN	POLAND	GHANA

No competition was held in 1940 or 1944 because of World War II.

COLLEGIATE TEAMS

Most universities and colleges with a sports program field a soccer team. Collegiate soccer utilizes most of the rules and strategies outlined in this book, with a few deviations for field size, substitutions, etc., and virtually all games are played outdoors on grass (as opposed to artificial turf). Please contact your local institutions directly, or contact the NCAA at 913-339-1906 to get more information on collegiate soccer in your area.

PROFESSIONAL LEAGUES
AND TEAMS—TICKET INFORMATION

The following is a list of the major professional soccer leagues in the U.S.—the APSL (OUTDOOR), the CISL (INDOOR) and the NPSL (INDOOR)—and their respective member teams. Please note that the INDOOR SOCCER leagues have various rule changes, most significantly the size of the playing field, which is close to the size of a hockey rink and includes walls rather than out of bounds lines.

Information on a new league (MLS, April 1995) is also included. Ticket information can be obtained by contacting the leagues or teams directly.

APSL

AMERICAN PROFESSIONAL SOCCER LEAGUE

The APSL's origins go back to February 12, 1989, with the announcement that the nation's two premier OUTDOOR SOCCER leagues, the Western Soccer League (WSL) and the American Soccer League (ASL), would work toward a merger. As planned, the two merged in February 1990, under the APSL banner and the league's inaugural interlocking season was 1991. While play on the field has continuously improved in quality, in the boardroom the League has substantially raised its standards of ownership—promising, and delivering, a much enhanced product.

TV: Information TBA

THE GAME: Traditional, full-field, outdoor soccer.

APSL League Office
3702 Pender Drive, Suite 210
Fairfax, VA 22030
Phone: (703) 273-PROS (7767)
Fax: (703) 273-9267
Founded: 1989

Colorado Foxes
6735 Stroh Road
Parker, CO 80134
Phone: (303) 840-1111
Fax: (303) 840-1238
Stadium: Mile High
(76,000)

Ft. Lauderdale Strikers
5301 NW 12th Avenue
Ft. Lauderdale, FL 33309
Phone: (305) 771-5677
Fax: (305) 491-3702
Stadium: Lockhart (9,500)

Houston Force
1200 Post Oak Boulevard,
Suite 200
Houston, TX 77056
Phone: (713) 529-5955
Fax: (713) 529-8088
Stadium: Robertson
(25,000)

Los Angeles Salsa
PO Box 6220
Fullerton, CA 92634-6220
Phone: (714) 547-2572
Fax: (714) 870-7070
Stadium: Titan (10,000)

Montreal Impact
8000 Langelier, Suite 104
St. Leonard, Quebec H1P
3K2 Canada
Phone: (514) 328-3668
Fax: (514) 328-1287
Stadium: Claude-Robillard
(8,000)

Seattle Sounders
1560 140th Avenue, NE,
Suite 200
Bellevue, WA 98005
Phone: (206) 622-3415
Fax: (206) 643-3515
Stadiums: Kingdome;
Memorial Stadium;
Tacoma Dome

Toronto Rockets
7135 Islington Avenue,
2nd Floor
Woodbridge, Ontario L4L
1V9 Canada
Phone: (905) 856-5511
Fax: (905) 856-5522
Stadium: Esther Shiner
Stadium (6,000)

Vancouver 86ers
1126 Douglas Road
Burnaby, B.C. V5C 4Z6
Canada
Phone: (604) 299-0086
Fax: (604) 299-1886
Stadium: Swangard
(6,500)

CONTINENTAL INDOOR SOCCER LEAGUE

The Continental Indoor Soccer League is the largest and most prominent professional soccer league in the United States. The CISL is backed by many powerful sports owners from the National Basketball Association and National Hockey League.

TV: The CISL is scheduled to televise 10-15 games on Prime Network during the 1994 season.

THE GAME: The excitement of INDOOR SOCCER begins with six players per side played on artificial turf within the confines of an ice hockey rink. Fast-paced action with "on-the-fly" substitution creates an eclectic atmosphere appealing to sports and entertainment enthusiasts. The length of a CISL game is approximately two hours.

CISL League Office
16027 Ventura Boulevard Suite 605
Encino, CA 91436
818/906-7627
818/906-7693 FAX

Arizona Sandsharks
201 E. Jefferson Street
Phoenix, AZ 85004
Phone: (602) 514-8300
Fax: (602) 514-8303

Dallas Sidekicks
Reunion Arena
777 Sports Street
Dallas, TX 75207
Phone: (214) 653-0200
Fax: (214) 748-0510

Anaheim (name TBA)
Arrowhead Pond of
Anaheim
2695 East Katella Ave.
Anaheim, CA 92806
Phone: (714) 704-2400
Fax: (714) 704-2443

Monterrey La Raza
Vasconcelos 715-A
Entre Genaro Garza y
Narango
GARZA GARCIA, Nuevo
Leon C.P. 66230
Mexico
Phone: 011 52
(83) 38-5669
Fax: 011 52
(83) 36-4728

Portland Pride
320 S.W. Stark, Suite
206
Portland, OR 97204
Phone: (800) 788-237
Fax: (503) 222-4939

Sacramento Knights
One Sports Parkway
Sacramento, CA 95834
Phone: (916) 928-0000
FAX: (916) 928-6919
San Diego Sockers
3942 Hancock Street
San Diego, CA 92110
Phone: (619) 224-4625
Fax: (619) 222-9020

Carolina Vipers
2700 Independence
Boulevard
Charlotte, NC 28205
Phone: (704) 343-CISL
(2475)
Fax: (704) 377-4595

Pittsburgh Stingers
Pittsburgh Civic Arena,
Gate 9
Pittsburgh, PA 15219-
3516
Phone: (412) 642-1800
Fax: (412) 642-1859

Las Vegas Dust Devils
105 E. Reno Avenue
Suite 4
Las Vegas, NV 89119
Phone: (702) 739-PROS
(7767)
Fax: (702) 739-1475

Houston Hotshots
The Interfin Building
1400 Post Oak Boulevard
Houston, TX 77056
Phone: (713) HOT-5100
Fax: (713) 840-0925

Detroit Neon
Two Championship Drive
Auburn Hills, MI 48326-
1752
Phone: (313) 377-0100
Fax: (313) 377-0981

Washington Warthogs
1 Harry S Truman Drive
Landover, MD 20785
Phone: (301) 499-3100
Fax: (301) 808-3015

San Jose Grizzlies
San Jose Arena
525 West Santa Clara St.
San Jose, CA 95113
Phone: (408) 971-SOCR
(7627)
Fax: (408) 999-5855

Seattle (1995)
800 Fifth Avenue
Suite 3770
Seattle, WA 98104
Phone: (206) 624-2888
Fax: (206) 623-7853

MLS
MAJOR LEAGUE SOCCER (APRIL, 1995)

Major League Soccer, a subsidiary of World Cup USA 1994, is a professional, outdoor soccer league planning to begin play in April of 1995. As the venture is a subsidiary of the World Cup USA 1994, it is related to FIFA (soccer's international governing body), which organizes the World Cup and the United States Soccer Federation (USSF), soccer's governing body in the U.S. and a member of FIFA.

The league plans to have twelve teams in various cities (to be announced) across the nation, and television coverage is expected. Inquiries about the fledgling league can be directed to the USSF at:

United States Soccer Federation
1801 S. Prairie Avenue
Chicago, IL 60616
Phone: (312) 808-9555

NATIONAL PROFESSIONAL SOCCER LEAGUE

The National Professional Soccer League (N.P.S.L.) is an INDOOR professional league dedicated to American players (more than 88 percent of its players are American citizens) and its American fans. The N.P.S.L. is the premier professional soccer league in the USA and in 1993-1994 celebrates its Tenth Anniversary Season. The league was formed in 1984 as the American Indoor Soccer Association but changed its name in 1990 to better identify itself with its national soccer/sports audience and corporate sponsors.

TV: ESPN and the NPSL have entered into a long-term partnership agreement to televise NPSL games on both ESPN and ESPN2.

THE GAME: The NPSL game is played on a hockey-sized rink with dasherboards and artificial turf, with the 8-foot-high by 14-foot-wide goals receded into the end zone dasherboards. The NPSL provides its fans with end to end action thanks to a multiple scoring system similar to basketball (1,2,3 point goals), and other rules designed for offensive play. Recent rule changes include shootouts and/or powerplay opportunites for certain time penalties; changing of players, including goalkeepers, on the fly; and over-and-back and 10-second delay rules for playing the ball out of the defensive zone.

National Professional Soccer League
229 Third St. NW
Canton, OH 44702
Phone: (216) 455-4625
Fax: (216) 455-3885
Founded: 1984

AMERICAN DIVISION

Baltimore Spirit
201 W. Baltimore Street
Baltimore, MD 21201
Phone: (410) 625-2320
Fax: (410) 625-2553
Stadium: Baltimore Arena
(12,392)

Buffalo Blizzard
140 Main Street
Buffalo, NY 14202
Phone: (716) 856-2500
Fax: (716) 852-3749
Stadium: Memorial
Auditorium (16,200)

Canton Invaders
1101 Market Avenue
North
Canton, OH 44702
Phone: (216) 455-6060
Fax: (216) 455-9000
Stadium: Canton Civic
Center (4,200)

Cleveland Crunch
34200 Solon Road
Solon, OH 44139
Phone: (216) 349-2090
Fax: (216) 349-0653
Stadium: CSU
Convocation Center
(12,493)

Dayton Dynamo
10561 Success Lane
Miamisburg, OH 45322
Phone: (513) 885-9551
Fax: (513) 885-3966
Stadium: Dayton
Convention Center (4,600)

Harrisburg Heat
PO Box 60123
Harrisburg, PA 17106
Phone: (717) 652-4328
Fax: (717) 233-8297
Stadium: State Farm Show
Arena (7,600)

Chicago Power
10850 Laraway Road
Frankfort, IL 60423
Phone: (708) 299-9000
Fax: (815) 469-2469
Stadium: Rosemont
Horizon (16,518)

Detroit Rockers
600 Civic Center Drive
Detroit, MI 48226
Phone: (313) 396-7574
Fax: (313) 396-7998
Stadiums: Cobo (9,561);
JLA (19,275)

Kansas City Attack
1800 Genessee
Kansas City, MO 64102
Phone: (816) 474-2255
Fax: (816) 474-8730
Stadium: Kemper Arena
(15,600)

Milwaukee Wave
6310 North Port
Washington Road
Milwaukee, WI 53217
Phone: (414) 962-9283
Fax: (414) 962-4837
Stadium: Bradley Center
(17,500)

St. Louis Ambush
5700 Oakland Avenue
St. Louis, MO 63110
Phone: (314) 647-1001
Fax: (314) 647-1002
Stadium: St. Louis Arena
(17,964)

Wichita Wings
319 So. Broadway
Wichita, KS 67202
Phone: (316) 262-3545
Fax: (316) 263-8631
Stadium: Kansas Coliseum
(9,681)

UNITED STATES SOCCER FEDERATION

NATIONAL GOVERNING BODY OF SOCCER (ALSO KNOWN AS THE USSF OR U.S. SOCCER)

United States Soccer Federation
1801 S. Prairie Avenue
Chicago, IL 60616
Phone: (312) 808-9555

The U.S. Soccer Foundation (USSF) or U.S. Soccer, has been a member of FIFA since 1913 and is the national governing body of soccer in the United States. Headquartered in Chicago, where the organization was relocated in December 1991, U.S. Soccer on July 4, 1988, was named the host national association for the 1994 World Cup.

The federation has 50 full-time employees working to administer and serve a membership located in all 50 states. It is a non profit, volunteer organization administered by a national council of elected representatives. Much of the federation's business is conducted by a 34-member board of directors representing three vast administrative arms—approximately 1.9 million youth players nineteen years of age and under; 220,000 senior players over the age of nineteen; and the professional division which oversees the sport at the professional level. The senior and youth divisions are divided into 51 and 55 state associations, respectively, with some states divided into two associations.

In addition to supervising and maintaining a registration system for thousands of players and referees, the federation also carries the responsibility of organizing national cup competitions, organizing and managing eight national teams that compete worldwide, arranging educational courses for players, coaches and referees, staging international matches and processing international player transfers.

NATIONAL SOCCER HALL OF FAME
(N.S.H.O.F.)

Oneonta, New York
Phone: (607) 432-3351

The National Soccer Hall of Fame is sanctioned by
F.I.F.A. and the U.S. Soccer Federation. It was designed
to promote a better understanding of soccer in America
through maintaining a historical record of soccer in the
United States, encouraging the involvement of youth in
the game and defining America's role in international
soccer.

The N.S.H.O.F. consists of the National Soccer Museum
and the 61-acre Wright National Soccer Campus. The
Campus has an exhibit hall that houses displays of
equipment and memorabilia from soccer's greatest players and teams as well as photos, artifacts, and trophy
cases filled with the sport's most sought-after prizes.
Clinics and tournaments are scheduled year-round, along
with special events, including soccer camps and work-
shops.

Founded: Although individuals have been inducted into
the Hall of Fame since 1950, the Hall was officially
established in 1979 and constructed in 1982.
Members: 191.

Publication(s): National Soccer Hall of Fame News
(bimonthly newsletter). $12.50 per year.

AYSO AMERICAN YOUTH SOCCER ORGANIZATION
"THE LEADER IN YOUTH SPORTS"

AYSO FACTS AND FIGURES

Name: The American Youth Soccer Organization (AYSO), a nonprofit organization.

Headquarters: AYSO's National Office in Hawthorne, California, provides services through a professional staff, Toll-free number: (800) USA-AYSO

West Office: (310) 643-6455.
FAX: (310) 643-5310.

Objective: Development of youngsters in body and character through the teaching and promotion of youth soccer.

Philosophy: Everyone Plays, Balanced Teams, Open Registration, Positive Coaching and Good Sportsmanship.

Affiliation: National Affiliate Member of the United States Soccer Federation.

Membership: Nearly 450,000 boys and girls, ages 5-18, nationwide, plus nearly 200,000 volunteer coaches, referees and administrators.

History: Founded in 1964 in Torrance, California, AYSO's revolutionary philosophy and unique approach to youth sports spread quickly. From nine teams in 1964 AYSO has grown to more than 30,000.

Registration Fee: Locally determined annual fee to include $7.50 per child to fund AYSO national services and United States Soccer Federation membership.

Structure: AYSO Regions (community programs) exercise local autonomy, operating within the Rules and Regulations and By-laws voted on by the Executive Membership.

Programs: AYSO offers coach and referee training and certification courses (from basic to advanced levels), administrative management seminars, player skills programs.

Major Services: AYSO provides computerized registration, Accident Reimbursement Plan, liability insurance, accounting plan, legal assistance and purchasing department.

Events: Tournaments, soccerfests, playoffs, clinics, volunteer meetings.

Publications: SOCCER NOW, full-color, quarterly magazine, distributed to all AYSO households, is the largest circulated soccer publication in the United States; IN-PLAY, quarterly newsletter for coaches and referees; AYSO Shorts, monthly newsletter.

US YOUTH SOCCER

"THE GAME FOR KIDS!"

Name: The United States Youth Soccer Foundation.

Headquarters: US Youth Soccer, 2050 North Plano Road, Suite 100 Richardson, Texas 75082 Toll-free number: 1-800-4-SOCCER (214) 235-4499, FAX: (214) 235-4480

Mission Statement: It is the mission of the United States Youth Soccer Association to foster the physical, mental and emotional growth and development of America's youth through the sport of soccer at all levels of age and competition. This association is established as a non profit and educational organization.

Area Covered: All fifty (50) states, including two National State Associations in the following states: California (North and South), New York (East and West), Ohio (North and South), Pennsylvania (East and West), Texas (North and South)

Players: Ages: Under 6 through Under 19 Sex: Male and Female Economic Background: All types Skill Level: Beginner to National Team

Sponsors: M&M Mars/Snickers: Title sponsor of the US Youth Soccer National Championship Adidas: Title sponsor of the US Youth Soccer Annual Workshop of Coaches Convention

Registration: 1,924,330 1992/93 registration as of 8/31/93

Publications: US Youth Soccer Newspaper—A quarterly publication jointly administered by US Youth Soccer and the Imperial Council of Shriners of North America, designed to connect local Shrine Temples and Shrine Clubs with local soccer teams. Shriners sponsor teams.

Promotional
Materials: 1) Youth Soccer Parent/Coach Primer;
2) Coaching U12 Player—Years of
Refinement (Continuation of the
Parent/Coach Series); 3) Assistant Coach
Series—U6 & U8 Activity Aids for the
Parent/Coach; 4) Assistant Coach Series—
U10 Activity Aids for the Parent/Coach;
5) Assistant Coach Series—U12 Activity
Aids for the Parent/Coach; 6) US YOUTH
SOCCER—The Game for Kids! Parents
Guide to US Youth Soccer; 7) The Official
US YOUTH SOCCER 3 v 3 Program;
8) Welcome to US YOUTH SOCCER...the
game for kids!; 9) Organizing a Recreation
Referee Program; 10) The Referee Mentor
Program; 11) The Boys Olympic
Development Program; 12) US YOUTH
SOCCER's Official Program for Young
People with Disabilities; 13) Developmental
Player Program Modified Playing
Guidelines U-6, U-8 & U10